HOT LEAD

ISSUE ONE

THE PICCADILLY COWBOYS

IN MEMORIA

THE PREMIERE ISSUE OF HOT LEAD IS DEDICATED TO TWO GIANTS OF THE WESTERN GENRE

BILL CRIDER... 1941—2018

It's always hard when friends depart for the untamed ranges beyond the Western veil. It is especially hard when they have been an integral part of your life and career for as long as you can remember. We lost such an individual this year. Bill Crider was a fine author, but more importantly, he was a good man who loved the written word, who never found a book he didn't want to take home, who was a mentor to many and a constant supporter of his peers. He was a man who brightened the day of all who came in contact with him. His knowledge of the Western genre was as wide and deep as his knowledge of mysteries, noir, and even science fiction. He was revered and appreciated by all. Shortly before his death, Bill provided an entry for this volume, as he had to the first volume in this series. To acknowledge his contributions and celebrate his lasting impact, this collection is dedicated to him. He is already missed.

DUSTY RICHARDS... 1937—2018

In January of this year Dusty Richards passed due to injuries suffered in a car wreck a month earlier. His wife, Pat, had passed a few days earlier, also from injuries suffered in the wreck. The author of more than 150 books, the 80 year old Western legend lived on Beaver Lake in the Ozarks of northwestern Arkansas. Dusty's trademark ten-gallon hat served him well in his many different roles, including renowned rodeo announcer, auctioneer, television and radio personality, entrepreneur, businessman, cattle farmer, cowboy, and master storyteller. However, he will be most remember by uncountable writers as a friend, teacher, and mentor. Described as an irresistible force and an unmovable object all rolled into one personality wider than the western skies he wrote about...an eternal optimist, a man who woke up each and every day renewed and ready for the next job, the next challenge, the next good fight, Dusty won numerous awards for his writing, including several prestigious Spur Awards from the Western Writers of America (WWA)—an organization he relentlessly promoted. Serving as President and a longtime board member of the WWA, Dusty believed in the power of the western novel, and in the power of WWA to promote the creatives behind the genre.

CONTENTS

Issue One
Published May 2018

Editor /writer
Justin Marriott

Ghost editor /writer
Paul Bishop

Additional Contributors
Andreas Decker
Steve Myall

Correspondence welcome
thepaperbackfanatic@sky.com

WEST OF PICCADILLY

THE PICCADILLY COWBOYS
BY PAUL BISHOP

The death knell of the Western genre was ringing loudly in the early 1970s, but then as tough a group of Brits as had never been west of the Mississippi, rode out of a dark and dangerous Piccadilly pub in the heart of London. Four deadly UK wordslingers with their battered typewriters tied down, ready to blast out paperbacks filled with violent, brutal, blistering action. They were set for a showdown against every tin star tradition of the western genre—and determined to shoot 'em to dollrags.

For the next decade, the gang known as The Piccadilly Cowboys carved more than three hundred notches on their combined typewriters—one for every hard, fast, ultra-violent tale they produced. Terry Harknett, Angus Wells, Laurence James, and John Harvey had truly never travelled west of London, yet their influence would save the western genre from obscurity.

Using assumed identities—pseudonyms such as George Gilman (Terry Harknett), William M. James (Harknett, Lawrence James, John Harvey), James A. Muir/Mathew Kirk (Angus Wells), L. J. Coburn (James, Harvey), and many others—these desperate men found inspiration in the filmatic violence, heat, dust, and bloodshed of Sergio Leone's spaghetti westerns. Together, they shunned the generic moral and puritanical principles of traditional westerns by splashing blood-soaked, nihilistic, hyper-realism across their pages.

Originally, the first of the Piccadilly Cowboys, Terry Harknett, took his inspiration from the shadowy and violent world of Morgan Kane, created by Norwegian bank clerk Kjell Hallbing. Under the pseudonym Louis Masterson, Hallbing depicting Kane as a hard-drinking, hard-living, guilt-ridden Texas Ranger. Beginning with *Without Mercy* in 1966, Kane galloped through more than 80 way-above-average adventures. The books were a phenomenal success in Hallbing's native Norway. Kane proved to be such a compelling character, he also made regular, shorter appearances in Arnesen's fortnightly

Western magazine. At the height of his popularity, there were even Morgan Kane playing cards!

Moving beyond Kane, the protagonists created by the Piccadilly Cowboys were not traditional anti-heroes, or even amoral drifters with their own personal code. They were often brutal, violent bullies—

EDGE IS A NEW KIND OF WESTERN HERO

EDGE
THE LONER

GEORGE G. GILMAN

No. 1

sociopathic villains—with no thought for anything beyond their own survival or the slaking of their depraved lusts—killing, vengeance, sadism, and prurient rutting. An output of over three hundred Westerns, in two dozen or more series featuring these vicious gunmen, cemented the reputation of the Piccadilly Cowboys for creating The Most Violent Westerns In Print...

ditional western—white-hatted, horse loving, damsel rescuers—reviled these blaggards, who they believed were destroying their legacy. When the frenzied pop-culture infatuation with the Vice Vice West eventually cooled, the custodians of conventional shoot-'em-ups celebrated. They were more than glad to let the Piccadilly Cowboys and their dark tales fade into the legends writers speak of with awe around the chuck wagon or campfire.

> AN OUTPUT OF OVER THREE HUNDRED WESTERNS CEMENTED THE REPUTATION OF THE PICCADILLY COWBOYS FOR CREATING THE MOST VIOLENT WESTERNS IN PRINT...

Despite having made the genre relevant again, these new neo-Westerns were not admired by everyone. The old guard of the tra-

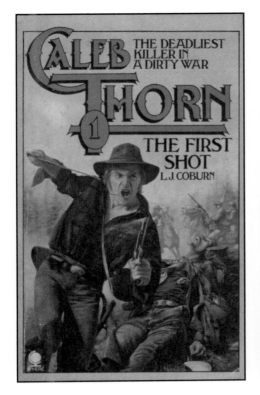

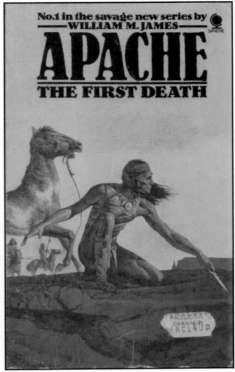

But, the traditionalists quickly learned they should be careful what they wished for. As the purists began to climb down from their high horses, they were blind-sided by a band of modern American word-slingers who started burning up the Western genre. Substituting the raw violence of the Piccadilly Cowboys with raw and raunchy sex of what would become known as Adult Westerns. The Western genre survived and eventually benefited from these sub-genres. Over time, however, the output of the Piccadilly Cowboys and the Adult Westerns have quietly been consigned to dusty corners in the darkest recesses of another dying breed—used paperback stores.

SUBSTITUTING THE RAW VIOLENCE OF THE PICCADILLY COWBOYS WITH RAW AND RAUNCHY SEX OF WHAT WOULD BECOME KNOWN AS ADULT WESTERNS

Today, the Western has matured into a six-guns blazing, style of storytelling combining time-honored themes and plots with the more modern sensibilities of deeper characterization and motivations. However, joining the current crop of Western scribes, is another group of upstart Brits. This time, however, they are not blazing

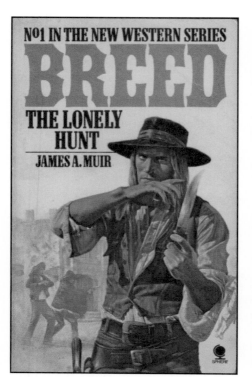

Nº1 IN THE NEW WESTERN SERIES

BREED

THE LONELY HUNT

JAMES A. MUIR

THEY CAME TO SELL GUNS—AND STAYED TO USE THEM!

GRINGOS 1

GUNS ACROSS THE RIVER

J D SANDON

JOHN B. HARVEY

HART

THE REGULATOR

JOHN WESLEY HARDIN

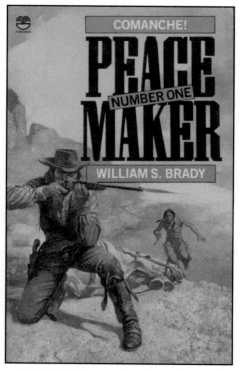

COMANCHE!

PEACE MAKER

NUMBER ONE

WILLIAM S. BRADY

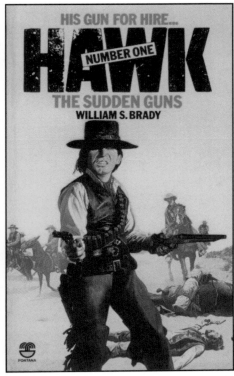

the trail of another exploitative Western sub-genre or stirring controversy.

Instead, writers such as Jo Walpole (the Maggie O'Bannen series under the pseudonym Jo Slade and other Westerns as Terry James), Andrew McBride (six novels in his Calvin Taylor series), and Ray Foster (numerous standalone westerns under the pseudonym Jack Giles) have embraced the Western with a genuine understanding of its current tenets and a healthy respect

> **WRITERS HAVE EMBRACED THE WESTERN WITH A GENUINE UNDERSTANDING OF ITS CURRENT TENETS AND A HEALTHY RESPECT FOR THE TRADITIONS THAT HAVE GONE BEFORE**

for the traditions that have gone before. Add in Australia's Kangaroo Cowboy, Brent Towns (aka: B.S. Dunn, Sam Clancy, Jake Henry, and Laramie Davis), and it becomes clear Wild West epics are continuing to be written from Piccadilly to the Outback, calling out homegrown Western wordslinger to a high noon showdown...

Issue Three: The Adult Westerns: Sex In The Saddle

A CHECKLIST OF PICCADILLY COWBOYS SERIES

Thanks to Steve Myall and Andreas Decker for their input.

Adam Steele
By George G Gilman
Second only to Edge, Steele lasted 49 episodes at New English Library from 1974 to 1989. Steele's early editions didn't benefit from the strong visual identity granted the Edge series by Richard Clifton-Dey until Tony Masero came on board. Pinnacle reprinted 26 in the US before their bankruptcy, with early covers alternating between Fred Love and George Gross.

Apache
By William M James
27 entries from 1974 to 1984. Co-created by Terry Harknett and Laurence James who alternated entries. With volume 15, Harknett left and John Harvey took over. Unusually for a Piccadilly Cowboys series, the complete run appeared only in the US courtesy of Pinnacle Books with covers by John Alvin and Bruce Minney. The series started at Sphere in the UK with four entries, and was reprinted over by New English Library who continued until volume twelve.

Breed
By James A Muir
A no-nonsense summary for a no-nonsense series – 22 books by Angus Wells from 1977 – 85 with UK editions only by Sphere Books. Some of the later titles in this series are tricky to track down.

Caleb Thorn
By L J Coburn
Relatively short-lived series of 5 books by John Harvey and Laurence James. Issued by Sphere in the UK in 1977 and 78, with no US paperback editions.

Claw
By Matthew Kirk
Angus Wells solo title, with 6 entries at Granada from 1983-84 with gritty painted covers from Roger Payne. No US editions.

Crow
By James W Marvin
Laurence James produced eight in this mini-series from 1979-82. See elsewhere in this issue for more.

Hart: The Regulator
By John B Harvey
Harvey flying solo for ten entries at Pan Books from 1980-82. Gino D'Achille provided the earthy covers which used Clint Eastwood as the inspiration/photo reference.

Edge
George G Gilman
The grand-daddy of the Piccadilly Cowboy series, Josiah Hedges had 61 adventures from 1972 to 1989. Pinnacle in the US reprinted 48, meaning there has been a demand for the final 13 which has driven up the cost of the UK editions. The visu-

al template for Edge set the standard for all other western series, with superb illustrations from Richard Clifton-Dey and Tony Masero.

Herne the Hunter
By John MacLaglen
24 entries from Laurence James and John Harvey at Corgi from 1976 – 84. Early covers were painted by Terry Gilbert with later ones by Chris Collingwood. Author Laurence James appears on a Collingwood cover as one of the lynch-men for *The Hanging*.

Gringos
By J D Sandon
Ten books at Mayflower from 1979 to 1982. Author duties split between John Harvey and Angus Wells. Painted covers by Richard Clifton-Dey featured characters from Sam Peckinpah's The Wild Bunch.

Gunslinger
By Charles C Garrett
Ten titles from Sphere in the UK from 1977 - 81, with books split between Laurence James and Angus Wells. First editions utilised an unusual cover style of featuring a close-up of a gun (a different gun was the theme of each episode) in the foreground. These were dropped for a series of reprints with art by Chris Collingwood which focused on figures with an Edge style lozenge for the title.

Hawk
By William S Brady
Angus Wells and John Harvey collaboration of 15 books from 1979-83. Published by Fontana in the UK with no US editions. Robert Adams painted the first 13 covers.

Jubal Cade
By Charles R Pike
22 entries from 1974 to 1983. Created by Terry Harknett who as at volume four gifted the series to Angus Wells to tempt him away from being an editor and to start writing. The only subsequent non-Wells entry was the eleventh, written by the versatile Ken Bulmer, but was such a disaster it was his only western. Published by Granada in the UK with painted covers by Richard Clifton-Dey. Chelsea House reprinted the first 13 for the American market.

Lawmen
By J B Dancer
John Harvey and Angus Wells delivered six entries for Coronet from 1977-80. I imagine it's one of this strange quirks, but all of my copies have been in shocking condition and I rarely see these in used bookstores.

Peacemaker
By William S Brady
Angus Wells and John Harvey, at Fontana UK for a nine-part series which started in 1981 and ended in 84. No US editions.

The Undertaker
By George G Gilman
Only six entries from Terry Harknett before this series was buried, published by NEL from 1981 to 82, with covers by Tony Masero. Pinnacle planned to reprint the series, but went bankrupt in 1985 after issuing only one title.

A NEW BREED OF WESTERN AUTHOR

AN INTERVIEW WITH TERRY HARKNETT THE CREATOR OF EDGE AND ADAM STEELE

Your first westerns were film novelisations for the New English Library. How did they lead to Edge?

Apparently at an editorial meeting with all of the New English Library board, Joe O'Leary said to Bob Tanner and Peter Haining, "All the spaghetti westerns are coming out and there are only books based on the films. Why don't we publish an original series?"

I knew Peter better back in these days, and it was he who said "Let's give it to Terry. I know he writes mysteries but he's written *Red Sun* and *Hannie Caulder* for us. Let's see if we can put him to work on a spaghetti western in print."

Tell me more about the development of Edge.

The first contract was for two books and as I thought these would be the only two. I wrote them and probably did certain things which I wouldn't if it knew it would run to 60 books!

Later, I started to put the books in a strict chronological timeframe but when I got to about number 20 Edge was starting to get too old to fit into that timeframe so they then began to get a bit wild and woolly in terms of realism. I think they were quite real when they started and the Civil War ones were well researched, but beyond that...

Whose idea were the puns at the end of each chapter in Edge?
It was entirely my idea. I had done a few novelisations of spaghetti westerns and they always had some grave- side hu- mour, so even thou gh that was miss- ing from the syn- opsis I work ed from, I actual- ly put that in. When I de- liv- ered the manu- script Peter Hain- ing

phoned me and said, "I like this, keep it going." So I made a rod for my own back as then I had to finish every chapter with a pun. Initially most of the puns came out of the story I was writing, but then I did start making a list of jokes which was a bit contrived because then you are working towards the pun rather than the character or the ac-

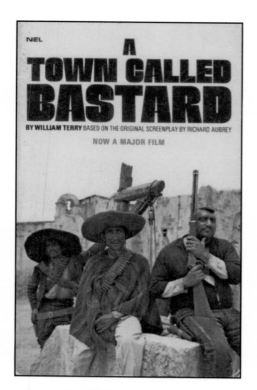

tion taking you there.   But it was fun and I enjoyed that aspect of it.

Was sex an editorial stipulation?
Sex was never an issue and my westerns didn't feature a lot of sex. The violence came about because they were born out of spaghetti westerns, and it was essential to keep it in that sub-genre.   It did bother me a bit because I'm not a violent person and I don't like violence on the screen.   In a book it doesn't bother me.   I hope I didn't go O.T.T. too often, although I did get some mail because I killed a child in one of the Edge books.

Were you ever any under pressure to outdo the sex and violence as the series moved on?
Never.   No-one suggested it but I softened the character because I was getting worried about the level of violence and started putting in more and more of these stupid jokes in to counter balance the violence. I just went with the flow. After the first two they then starred commissioning them in blocks of four.   The longer it went, the easier it became, until towards the end when it was obvious sales were going down and I was losing interest in them.   I started to ask myself whether I had written 60 books, or one book 60 times.

When did you realise the novels were big-sellers?
NEL phoned me and told me the first two are selling like hot cakes and so we'll give you a contract for another four.   When those four sold equally as well it snowballed.

Although it wasn't my genre of choice I just went with it and I did get plenty of crime in there – admittedly Mickey Spillaine rather than Raymond Chandler.

The packaging and design of the Edge books was undoubtedly helping their success.
Ceil Smith headed up the art department. He was a nice guy but I never had a lot to do with him. On the cover art of my books, I cannot thank Dick Clifton-Dey, another late and very much lamented friend and colleague, enough for how he created the image of Edge that lives in the minds of the fans.

I never saw Dick at the NEL offices, it was only at our yearly 'Hacks Lunch'. I never had any reason to speak to Dick unless it was socially and invariably we were both smashed out of our minds. Him more than me! I remember after one year I got a phone call to say Dick's wife has found him in a tree in their back garden and he won't come down. As far as I know he stayed up there all night!

Couldn't fault his covers, if it hadn't been for Dick creating that image which stuck with people, the series would not have been as successful. Until then no western series had an identifiable character on the cover. They were all generic and interchangeable – I know they were because I used to work for a features agency which used to buy transparencies of western covers from Australia to put on totally different

westerns published here by Brown Watson.

Dick used to phone me up and ask what I was going to put in the next book and if there was any particular scene I wanted picked out. Occasionally he would ask me to change a locale – have a fight on a street rather than a bar, for instance. He always did the pictures terrifically but stopped because NEL weren't paying him enough money and was getting an awful lot of ads in the Sunday supplements.

UNTIL THEN NO WESTERN SERIES HAD AN IDENTIFIABLE CHARACTER ON THE COVER.

So what happened then?

This left a gap that it took NEL a time to fill adequately as they experimented with a number of artists and there were a couple of really horrendous covers that were put out. When Tony Masero came on the scene and stayed I was very pleased. He did a marvellous thing in that he was a superb commercial artist but he didn't have any pretensions and was happy to match his style to Dick's without feeling as if he had lowered his sights.

Not only did he produce, in my opinion, consistently fine work in

the style of another (something I'm sure is hard for an artist to do) but we often had interesting telephone conversations after he had seen the synopses for new books I had submitted to NEL. During these discussions we would exchange ideas for what scenes Tony should depict and which characters should be on the covers.

Tell me more about the development of the Adam Steele series.
Steele was based on a film script. Laurence had got involved with this guy called Howard Brandy for someone called Group Faberge and we visited their very plush set of offices just off Park Lane. I remember they had white fur carpets everywhere! Brandy said, "We like

your books, please write a film script for us."

I'd been told before that the best part of my books was the dialogue and I knew what a film script looked like as I had worked for 20th Century Fox for a while. Apparently the script I delivered was too expensive to film as it would involve far too many sets and scenes. I was never one to waste anything, so when NEL asked me to do a companion series to Edge, I turned the script into the first Steele adventure.

I went for the obvious option in that Edge fought for the Union, Steele for the Confederacy, and physically they looked differently. The on-

ly thing they shared was the dark humour. Steele was always second string but I found the work refreshing and I'm sure if I was just doing Edge I would have gone stale a lot more quickly than I did. There's only so much you can get out of a character as he progresses through life.

Edge was actually commissioned for a movie at one point?

That's tragic. It shows me under a bad light as an idiot. It was put under option by Irving Allen.

The Irwin Allen who made the big-budget disaster movies? That's the mistake I made! This was another chap. This Irving Allen produced a couple of westerns in Germany/Spain and paid me £500 a year to option the whole series as

> STEELE WAS ALWAYS SECOND STRING BUT I FOUND THE WORK REFRESHING

Photo from National Newsagent magazine. Caption- "Success for former NN deputy editor Terry Harknett! Recently New English Library held a reception in the Waldorf Hotel, London, to celebrate the milliomth copy sold of Edge - a runaway popular Western series written by Terry, better known to his Edge fans as George G Gilman. To mark the occasion NEL's managing director, presented Terry with a leather bound copy of the first title in the Edge series - The Loner - and the original art work, framed, from one of the front covers. "

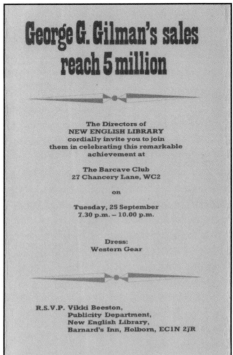

long as it was running. I thought, lovely, but while he had that option no-one else could do anything, and it only finished when the series did. Of course, no-one wanted to make a film by then.

Same with Edge's US publishers Pinnacle going bust, and according to US law no-one could publish their books until a year after they had gone into receivership. By the time that year was up, the western had died and no-one was interested in the books.

How were you coping with the deadlines?
The shortest time it took me to write a book was a little over a week but after the initial crazy days of signing contracts left, right and centre were over and I settled down to produce four Edge and four Adam Steele titles a year they each took about a month. This allowed four months annually for other things. And during some of this 'spare' time I would work on the synopses for new books. And I submitted these four at a time to NEL on a regular basis when they asked for them - usually quite early so they could plan their publishing schedules.

NEL were not known for their generosity....
For the first Edge book they paid a £150 advance and offered 4.5% royalties. About half of what most mainstream publishers paid! That's why I became so prolific.

After I gave up my post at the National Newsagent to start writing fiction full time. I said to my wife Jane, "If I don't earn as much in that year as I would on the paper, I'll go back there". I made it by about £20!

At what point did NEL renegotiate your contract?

As we approached number 50 in the Edge series, I said this is ridiculous. So for the last two or three contracts they were paying me £1000 a book, £330 on signature, £330 on delivery and £330 upon publication. There were lots of foreign editions that paid piddling amounts, until the Americans at Pinnacle came in with a much bigger advance and bigger royalties.

> I SAID TO MY WIFE JANE, IF I DON'T EARN AS MUCH IN THAT YEAR AS I WOULD ON THE PAPER, I'LL GO BACK THERE. I MADE IT BY ABOUT TWENTY POUND!

Western fans were notorious for picking up historical inaccuracies....

Almost without exception, all the mail I received was very flattering and admiring. One of the Edge a stories has a cage made of gold and put on the back of the wagon, and I had a letter from a university student stating it would have taken an articulated lorry to shift a cage made of gold! The key is getting your guns right. If you get your guns right the readers will forgive you all.

What was the reaction of the traditional western authors to your new school of spaghetti pulps?

I never came into contact with any Western writers who were not within the circle of the so-called Piccadilly Cowboys and since they were all in the same hard-boiled school there was never any friction among us concerning the old style-new school.

I did hear long ago that J.T. Edson was most upset when a tabloid newspaper ran a feature that alleged I and a number of other writers new to the genre had made uncomplimentary remarks about Mr Edson and others of his ilk and their style of writing. This article was based upon entirely fictitious 'interviews' with we new boys and so was no more than an exercise in trouble making. Nothing came of it as far as I know and as is the way with daily newspaper articles of no real import it was forgotten as soon as the journal concerned was used to wrap fish-and-chips the following day.

Did you and the Piccadilly Cowboy writers ultimately destroy the market by flooding it with too many books?

Yes I think so. We walked into it with our eyes wide open because it

Continued on page 25

BILL TIDY ON EDGE

Reprinted from Punch magazine, April 1974. Bill Tidy was a well known cartoonist.

"Edge is a new kind of Western hero," it says on the outside of the book. On the inside, he is 6 foot 3 inches tall, weighs 190lbs. (Some bone, mostly muscle), is hook-nosed, firm-jawed and has light piercing blue eyes.

Yes, that's reasonable. We all know that the old kind of Western hero was 5 foot 5 ½ inches tall, built like a pile of bricks, short-sighted, and chinless. Edge is bent on revenge. (Indians were partly responsible for the death of his freshly picked wife) and he's fast with a Henry repeating rifle. He murmurs "Obliged" to ladies.

Oh, come on, Edge, what's so new about you? You're just like all the other White Hats. You don't say much, served for the North agin the South, the farm run by your crippled brother burns down as you are on your way home, the pouch between your shoulder blades containing the honed razor which you lace people-

Hello! I don't recollect heroes carrying razors. Even in the worst saloon brawl, as the bartender sank behind the counter, clutching his best two bottles, and the mirror with the engraving of Lili Langtry collapsed, only the baddie ever produced a knife or a razor.

But Edge, ex-Captain Josiah Hedges, is what heroes have putrefied to as a result of our present lust affair with violence.

The level of cruelty in the Edge books (There at least ten titles and near 1 ½ million sold), makes them a certainty, I'm sorry to say, for the cinema.

He's called Edge because a Mexican dropped the "H" in terror and the name stuck. He is a sadist, and worse still has no sense of humour. Our hero is given to the James Bond habit of making feeble mots at sick moments. A vulture staggers backward as it tugs at something which suddenly comes free from one of Edge's deceased mates. As the bird lurches into the sky the entrails of Bob Rhett can be seen swinging from its bill. Edge grinned, "You never did have any guts, Bob." Bond at his most post-coital was never as limp as that.

Victims of Edge's razor, revolver, knife and pump action Henry repeater rifle die in a fine spray. The arc of a knife and the trajectory of a bullet are the hors d'oeuvre for a twenty course meal of gore. Even the brothel scene in Edge The Loner can't be honest grumble and grunt. One cad at work with a bored girl still wears "filthy under-vest and pants open where it had proved necessary." Bearing in mind the atmosphere of the book, I'd expect him to have a button-up armpit. Sioux Uprising has our New Western Hero focusing a burning glass in a nasty old man's forehead. It's cruel, vicious and repetitive apart from a decapitated sheriff's head being carried off by a slavering hound. That only happens once.

Am I over-reacting to what is bread and butter today? Violence and brutishness never left this place. You don't have to buy books dedicated to sadism, and it's only pretend and anyway the Western needed a change. Maybe, but the Edge books shocked me. I've seen the Western grow up. In every Western there was always a laugh. I can't imagine anyone laughing Edge's company, unless his throat was doing it for him, gaping and rhythmically pumping out a bubbling broth. Edge's lips drew back in a mirthless chuckle. "Always said red was your colour."

MORE FROM THE EDGE FAN CLUB...

"Josiah Hedges, hero of a long strong of Edge books by George G Gilman is an affirmative Action killer. Before getting very deeply into The Loner, we learn that Hedges has personally killed 56 people. Then, in the opener, he kills another 16 including two kids who were harassing him and one woman."

"In addition to the ordinary hardware of a gun-man, Hedges carries a bone-handled hunting knife in a sheath at the small of his back and a long, slim pouch hanging down his back from a thong about his neck. The pouch carries a razor which he uses with flourishes, disfiguring faces, slicing through jugular veins, and like that. He has a lot of hate, does Josiah Hedges, and we have a lot of it for this series in which we have been unable to detect a single redeeming feature."

"Pinnacle Books has earned a reputation for pioneering, practically, "series" titles such as Edge, Fox, the Executioner, the Destroyer, the Butcher, etc. Some of them are excellent: Fox, for example, and Hazard, Sherdian and the reprints of Hornblower. The rest are on a par with pornography of the hard-core variety and it is creepy trying to figure out who is gobbling up these books. We're probably better off not knowing."

Paperback Rack by Dale L Walker, The El Paso Times

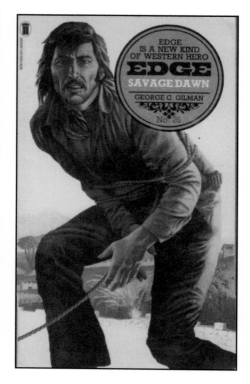

was easy to do. We worked hard at it. Well, I certainly did and tried to make them as original as we could but there were too many and they were very samey.

I never read any. I've always maintained that the reason my books were original was because I had never read a western. I had seen all the movies and TV series but I had never read one. So thankfully I hit an original streak and it captured the hearts and minds of a lot of people. Thank God!

I'VE ALWAYS MAINTAINED THAT THE REASON MY BOOKS WERE ORIGINAL WAS BECAUSE I HAD NEVER READ A WESTERN.

Let's imagine an alternate history where the spaghetti westerns had flopped ... I wouldn't have been in the publishing industry if that had happened. I think I proved I couldn't write saleable mysteries and I wouldn't have followed the westerns off my own back. I would have stayed in journalism, probably for the trade press, scraping a living through writing with my pen or my electronic typewriter with a daisy wheel!

As Terry Harknett discusses in his interview, New English Library (N.E.L.) searched for a replacement for Edge cover artist Clifton-Dey with mixed success before selecting Tony Masero. Clifton-Dey never illustrated Steele, and it was primarily Bill Francis Phillips who portrayed Steele before Masero got the gig, as shown on this page.

The opposite page shows example of Edge between Clifton-Dey and Masero. Bottom left is Francis Phillips. The other three are probably the work of Ray Feibush who was often employed to imitate the style of other artists by NEL. Their visuals more readily show Charles Bronson as the model for Edge.

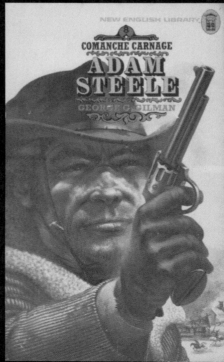

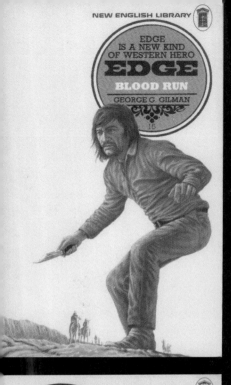

NEW ENGLISH LIBRARY

EDGE IS A NEW KIND OF WESTERN HERO

EDGE

BLOOD RUN

GEORGE G. GILMAN

16

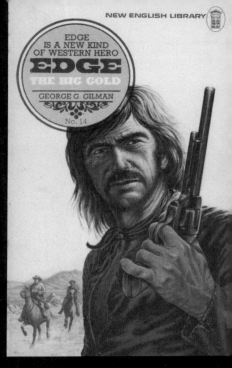

NEW ENGLISH LIBRARY

EDGE IS A NEW KIND OF WESTERN HERO

EDGE

THE BIG GOLD

GEORGE G. GILMAN

No. 14

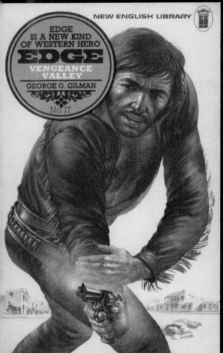

NEW ENGLISH LIBRARY

EDGE IS A NEW KIND OF WESTERN HERO

EDGE

VENGEANCE VALLEY

GEORGE G. GILMAN

No. 17

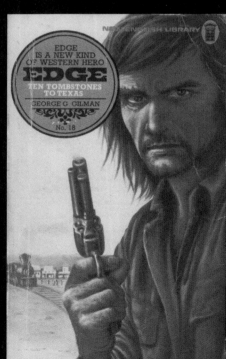

NEW ENGLISH LIBRARY

EDGE IS A NEW KIND OF WESTERN HERO

EDGE

TEN TOMBSTONES TO TEXAS

GEORGE G. GILMAN

No. 18

A VIOLENT MAN IN A VIOLENT LAND

HERNE THE HUNTER
BY JUSTIN MARRIOTT

Herne the Hunter, rather mischievously named after an English figure of folk-lore, was one of the longer-running series penned by the Piccadilly Cowboys, running for twenty-four adventures at Corgi Books from 1976 to 1984. It was produced tag-team style by experienced editor recently turned freelance writer Laurence James and a rapidly developing John Harvey. Of course, many of you will recognise James as the man who took the Deathlands series to great heights for Gold Eagle and Harvey for his polemical Resnick crime novels.

But this was much earlier in their careers, with their words raw and racing out of an over-heated typewriter in a race against deadlines, with plots and ideas foraged like a Magpie from wider popular culture, including a sword and sorcery novel anti-hero and a notorious horror film. As a result, the Herne series has an off-beat and genre-subverting nature which won't be to everyone's tastes. Which might explain why there were no American editions, despite James enjoying a strong working relationship with Andy Ettinger at Pinnacle Books, who were already successfully reprinting other UK originated series from the Piccadilly Cowboys, specifically

Edge and Steele. And other series from James, such as The Killers (by Klaus Nettson in the US), and The Gladiators (by Andrew Quiller, collaborating with Ken Bulmer).

In White Death, the 1976 opener, the reader is introduced not to the legendary gun-slinger Herne the Hunter but one Jebediah Travis Herne—middle-aged, greying at the temples, his holsters gathering dust as he attempts to eke out a peaceful existence as a humble farmer. Depicting a gunman looking to replace the bloodstains on his hands with that of toiled mud strikes me as great way of differentiating the tone of the series to others.

Of course, Herne must return to the way of the gun as presumably the pitch for Herne the Farmer didn't do well with

research groups. The trigger point is the suicide of his young wife following her ordeal when seven drunken misfits are dumped by a passing train. Having discovered her swinging from the rafters, a scene depicted for the cover by artist Terry Gilbert with Eastwood cast as the taciturn anti-hero, Herne

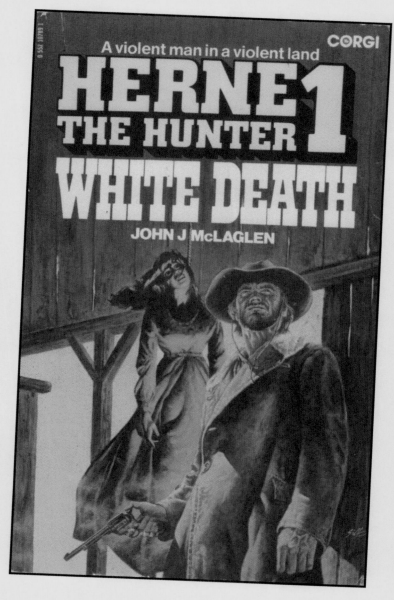

dusts off his guns, sharpens his boot-bayonet and embarks on the compulsory vendetta.

Joining Herne's on his mission for rough justice are neighbour William Yates and his teenage daughter Rebecca, who also suffered at the hands of the seven. This is a short-lived association when Yates predilection for torturing prostitutes is revealed and he's promptly executed by Herne. Rebecca becomes Herne's sole responsibility and at this stage the series unwisely adopted an unsavoury sub-plot fo-

HERNE DUSTS OFF HIS GUNS, SHARPENS HIS BOOT-BAYONET AND EMBARKS ON THE COMPLUSORY VENDETTA

cussing on Rebecca's budding sexuality and her feelings for Herne.

After temporarily being sent off to a private school (where after only one night she falls victim to the perverted head-mistress who flogs her and then attacks her using a pair of tailor-made sharpened metal teeth!) Rebecca is shipped off to Europe by Herne, returning only to die of tuberculosis in book seven *Death Rites* (1978).

Following the departure of Rebecca, Herne's interaction with the

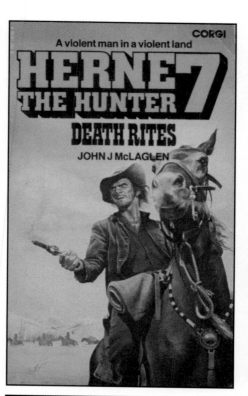

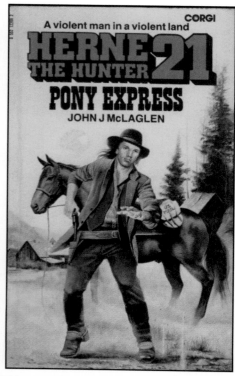

fairer sex was thankfully restricted to brief encounters with those above the age of consent, typically whore with hearts of gold or frustrated wives neglected by their fat rancher husbands.

On a more positive note, the Herne series had a stronger continuity than its peers, including recurring characters such as Herne's nemesis; Whitey Coburn, an albino bounty-hunter with gun-fighting skills to rival Herne's. Albino's were a recurring feature of James' books and undoubtedly a nod of the head in the direction of Elric, the albino and drug-addicted 'anti-Conan' invented by Michael Moorcock.

Although Coburn was supposedly killed by Herne in the aptly named *The Black Widow* (1977), he returned in *Death in Gold* (1977), and more notably for *Massacre* (1978). The latter being a 'flashback' episode which explained their feud. Whitey also played a very small part in a later 'flashback' entry, *Pony Express (1983)*.

In my view, *Massacre!* is the standout in the series. Helped by the innovative flashback technique, it effectively utilised the atrocities committed by Quantrill's Raiders, a gang of rogue Confederate troops who became outlaws in the aftermath of the Civil War.

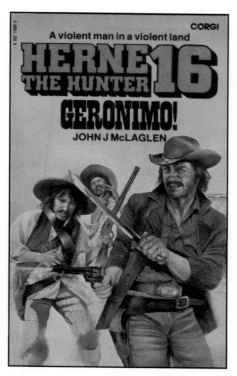

Other entries which carried a historical core were *Geronimo* (1981) and Harvey's finest contribution to the series, *Billy the Kid* (1980).

In the hands of James in particular, Herne was a truly grim series, macho and sadistic beyond belief. In one anecdote in the opening to a book, it relays how a horse-trader reneged on a deal with Herne to return a prize stallion from horse-nappers. In return Herne kidnaps his wife who is then discovered alive, but with ears, little fingers and toes removed! The prevailing atmosphere is one of unrelenting doom with very few characters displaying any redeeming features, let alone surviving to the end of a book.

Of course it's violent, with the required descriptions of shattered cheek-bones and jellied eye-balls served up every few chapters, but it's the ludicrous XXX-pantomime villains that make some of the Herne books unforgettable. Such as Jesus a sadistic Mexican dwarf who sodomises his unfortunate male captives (a friend of mine tells me there was a dwarf of that name that appeared in 1970s porn films, so possibly an in-joke typical of Laurence James), and opium addicted twins who share an incestuous relationship with their bondage-loving mother! Sick, sick, sick, and evidently an author having a ball trying to shock his editors, fellow authors and readers.

James and Harvey further subverted the genre by chucking in imagery and themes ripped from other genres of popular culture. *Texas Massacre* (1984) is a prime example, with James recreating a late 19th century version of notorious horror film *The Texas Chainsaw Massacre* (1974) with the setting relocated to Virginia.

By upping the gore and kink to such extreme levels it was inevitable that the audience for the Herne

----

IT'S THE LUDICROUS XXX-PANTOMIME VILLAINS THAT MAKE SOME OF THE HERNE BOOKS UNFORGETTABLE.

----

books would narrow. I can't imagine too many western readers, even those whose blood-lust was typically catered for by the Piccadilly Cowboys, picking up *Texas Massacre* and thinking this is a series they would continue to seek out.

Possibly James and Harvey were aware of this, and had either anticipated the collapse of the PC genre or were being tempted away by new commissions, so decided to go out with a last hurrah by cramming in all of the off-beat influences they could whilst having an absolute blast. They certainly succeeded. Readers with cast-iron stomachs and a sick sense of humour looking for an anti-hero will find themselves well served by Herne.

HERNE THE HUNTER CHECKLIST

Laurence James and John Harvey
as John McLaglen
Corgi Books, UK

1. *White Death*, 1976, Laurence James
2. *River of Blood*, 1976, John Harvey
3. *The Black Widow*, 1977, Laurence James
4. *Shadow of the Vulture*, 1977, John Harvey
5. *Apache Squaw*, 1977, Laurence James
6. *Death in Gold*, 1977, Harvey
7. *Death Rites*, 1978, Laurence James
8. *Cross-Draw*, 1978, Harvey
9. *Massacre!* 1978, Laurence James
10. *Vigilante!* 1979, John Harvey
11. *Silver Threads*, 1979, Laurence James
12. *Sun Dance*, 1980, John Harvey
13. *Billy the Kid*, 1980, John Harvey
14. *Death School*, 1980, Laurence James
15. *Till Death*, 1980, John Harvey
16. *Geronimo*, 1981, Laurence James
17. *The Hanging*, 1981, Laurence James
18. *Dying Ways*, 1982, John Harvey
19. *Bloodline*, 1982, Laurence James
20. *Hearts of Gold*, 1982, John Harvey
21. *Pony Express*, 1983, Laurence James
22. *Wild Blood*, 1983, John Harvey
23. *Texas Massacre*, 1984, Laurence James
24. *The Last Hurrah!* 1984, Laurence James

THE COWPOKE CRITIC

Steve Myall's regular reviews column for Hot Lead debuts with a look at the Piccadilly Cowboys.

APACHE #1:
THE FIRST DEATH
By William M. James
Pinnacle, 1974

Pinnacle published George G. Gilman's very successful Edge series in America and saw them agree to publish a new series written by the man behind the Gilman pseudonym, Terry Harknett, and Laurence James. The series idea came from the latter. Both these English authors, alongside a couple of others would later become known as the Piccadilly Cowboys. When Terry decided to stop writing for this series his place was taken over by John B. Harvey, another of the PCs. The series ran from 1974 to 1984 and saw the publication of 27 books. Only the first 12 were published in the authors' home country. The first book I'm reviewing here being written by Terry Harknett.

This opening novel deals with the misunderstandings that lead to the tragic deaths that will set Cuchillo on the vengeance trail in the following books. It also explains how he gets his new name, Cuchillo Oro, and how he comes to carry the bejewelled knife.

> THE BOOK IS SUPERBLY PACED, FULL OF WELL-CRAFTED CHARACTERS AND SAVAGE BLOODY ACTION.

The book is superbly paced, full of well-crafted characters, and savage bloody action. There aren't any white-hat heroes here, just hard men, and women, struggling to survive. Sympathies lie with the Apaches, as to be expected in a series with one of them as the lead character, and the soldiers are painted, mainly, as vicious, heartless, men who think nothing of torturing and raping, who take great pleasure from doing this, so it isn't long before the reader is urging Cuchillo to victory. There is one white man who is a friend of Cuchillo, teacher John Hedges, a man who will turn up from time to time in later books.

to get the greatest enjoyment from them.

BREED #15:
SLAUGHTER TIME
as by James A. Muir
Sphere, 1981

Angus Wells, writing as James A. Muir, once again proves that he wrote some of the most savage books that came from the pen of the Piccadilly Cowboys. This book is filled with brutal men – Azul included – and moves from one violent confrontation to another at a rapid pace.

Wells writes confidently and his attention to detail is exceptional, be it about the land, the heat, or

For those who've read the Edge books and are aware of the groan worthy, grin-making, one liners of gallows humour Terry Harknett always included you'll be pleased to discover he continues that tradition here, not as often but just as good, or bad, depending on your point of view.

The book ends with a very violent rescue attempt that leads to a couple of horrific killings that sees the story end with a promise that paves the way to the next book in the series and will leave you wanting more.

Due to its continuing storyline I'd suggest reading the books in order

the effects of bullets against flesh and bone, and of dying – read the description of teardrops into sand to see what I mean.

Breed comes across as single-minded, nothing will stop him achieving his need for revenge. At times he seems cold-hearted; witness the torture scene in the sand-pit – savage yes but very memorable, and not one drop of blood spilled.

Like many of the Piccadilly Cowboys, Wells makes plenty of references to some of the other writers, their heroes, and those from films. Here you get mention of a romantic book written by Loretta James (Laurence James), Chato's hunt for revenge (Charles Bronson's film *Chato's Land*), a book called *Gunlaw* by Charles Garrett (the pseudonym used for the Gunslinger books about a gunsmith), and there's reference to the book Edge #14: *The Big Gold* (*Tiger's Gold* in America), when a girl remembers being taken to see a travelling carnival and its block of gold protected by a tiger – she likens Breed to a hunting tiger.

This rates as one of my favourite books in the Breed series and, if you like the more brutal type of westerns, then you should consider tracking down a copy.

JUBAL CADE #17: BLOODY CHRISTMAS
as by Charles R. Pike
Granada, 1981

The Jubal Cade series was created by Terry Harknett – perhaps better known as George G. Gilman – but he only wrote the first three before handing the series over to Angus Wells, who wrote all but one of the other books, that odd book (#11) being written by Ken Bulmer. In total the series ran for 22 books, first appearing in 1974 with the final book being published in 1983.

> ALL OF THE CADE BOOKS SHOWCASE THE SUPERB WORK OF THE LATE RICHARD CLIFTON-DEY AND THIS ONE REALLY DOES SHOW HIS UNDERSTANDING OF THE USE OF LIGHT, SHADE AND COLOUR.

In my mind the Jubal Cade books had one of the best tag lines ever used to sell a western series, if not the best ever: "A man trained to heal – but born to kill."

Bloody Christmas begins with Cade still searching for the man who killed his wife and it's hearing that the Farrin's offer a safe haven to outlaws that brings Cade to them to see if they've heard of the man he is hunting, Lee Kincaid.

The Farrin's offer to help Cade find Kincaid if he first uses his medical skills to deliver Alice Farrin's baby. The fact that the mother insists they need a doctor present to deliver the child starts the alarm bells ringing. This isn't the only mystery surrounding this birth. The Farrin's

A WINTER WORLD OF VIOLENT DEATH

JUBAL CADE

BLOODY CHRISTMAS

17

CHARLES R. PIKE

refuse to tell Cade who the father is. And why is one end of the large homestead kept locked and in darkness, even though the fire is kept burning?

At first Cade wants nothing more than to leave the Farrin's but the winter weather closes all trails out and soon Cade's curiosity gets the better of him and he wants answers to his questions.

The truth is slowly revealed and it's here that Angus Wells adds themes one would expect to find in a horror book more than in a western. The Farrin's secret leading to some extremely detailed killings that at times are described over more than one page per death. Of course, this kind of attention to vio-lent death is to be expected from a book from the Piccadilly Cowboy's stable – and Angus Wells' work in particular.

This a well told story, with most of the action taking place on Christ-mas Eve and Christmas Day, that seamlessly combines elements of horror with the western to provide the reader with a gripping and sav-age read.

I'd also like to comment on the cov-er art. All of the Cade books show-case the superb work of the late Richard Clifton-Dey and this one really does show his understanding of the use of light, shade and col-our, so not only do you get a great read you also get a terrific cover too.

CLAW #1:
DAY OF FURY
as by Matthew Kirk
Granada, 1983

Blacksmith Tyler Wyatt was not a man to go looking for trouble, but trouble found him the day Vance Jennings and his gang hit town. They took away his wife, his home…and his left hand. They gave him in return a searing lust for death and revenge that nothing – no matter how bloody – could ev-er satisfy.

This series was the last to come from The Piccadilly Cowboys, and Angus Wells wrote all six books.

Like most of the western series

from this group of authors the first book sees the hero's happy life destroyed and him setting out on the revenge trail.

The book begins with Wyatt about to torture and kill a lawman in his quest to track down and kill Jennings and his gang. How Wyatt came to be on this vengeance trail is told in a series of flashbacks, which form the major part of this story, the book ending not that much further into the future than were it began. Like all good serials this one doesn't see Wyatt fulfilling his mission to kill all the men who wronged him, thus ensuring you'll buy the next book to see what happens next.

Angus Wells probably wrote the most descriptive books when it came to the actual killings and brutality than any of the other PC authors and, with this series, he perhaps out-does even himself. Many of the violent acts, be they rape, torture, or killing, are depicted in savage detail, often taking a couple of pages to describe. The destruction of Wyatt's hand and its subsequent amputation being cases in point. Having Wyatt replace his hand with a claw allows Wells to write even more gruesome death scenes as this is Wyatt's preferred weapon for dealing out his form of justice.

The story moves swiftly from one bloody act to another and it's interesting to observe the changes Wyatt goes through as each new horror befalls him and those he loves. Jennings and his gang are equally well drawn and the book sets up the revenge theme that will continue over the course of the next two books extremely well.

I always thought it a shame the cover artist, Roger Payne, didn't paint the claw a little more like it's described by Angus Wells but it's not that far off.

Due to the extreme graphic violence the Claw series won't be to everyone's tastes but if you like the other PC westerns then I'd say it's a safe bet that you'll enjoy this one too.

CROW #1: THE RED HILLS
By James W. Marvin
Corgi, 1979

The Crow series was written by the late Laurence James, who as one of the Piccadilly Cowboys, perhaps authored the most twisted and sadistic books of them all.

With Crow, James created the coldest anti-hero than any of the others came up with. A man that is very hard to like, yet because of this becomes a fascinating character. How can anyone really like a man, who when we first meet him, kills a child's pet dog in front of her simply because it took his scarf and the girl couldn't get it back fast enough for him?

Even if Crow comes across as a heartless and vicious character then what of Silas Menges? The

shocking killing of the dog and from then the pace doesn't let up. We don't learn much about Crow's past as he prefers not to discuss it, although at one time he does reveal some events from his past, but you're never quite sure if what he says is true or just said to shock. The fight scenes are filled with blood and descriptive deaths and the body count is high, leading to a savage final torturous confrontation.

The Crow books aren't going to appeal to all western readers, but for those who like anti-heroes and stories filled with brutal killing then this series is definitely worth hunting for.

Captain is portrayed superbly and almost makes Crow seem like a warm and caring man. Menges' foul mouth and demented beliefs soon having the reader hoping Crow kills him sooner rather than later.

Like many of the anti-heroes created by the Piccadilly Cowboys, Crow carries unusual weapons, a sawn down Purdey shotgun carried in a hip holster and a cut down sabre. Both are used to devastating effect.

The book starts, like all the Crow books, with a reporter asking an old man to relate tales about Crow. Both reporter and the old man are unnamed. The next chapter goes back in time and brings forth the

EDGE #21: RHAPSODY IN RED
as by George G. Gilman
NEL, January 1977

High Mountain, a small frontier town in Colorado, is to stage a musical extravaganza and wild festival. Rollo Stone, the famous violinist, is the main attraction and hordes of music lovers pack the town to witness the event. But with crowds comes trouble. The fragile rule of law and order collapses as a bunch of hired guns take over. The sheriff is gunned down and Edge, forever in the thick of things, is left to sort out the mess.

The main theme of this book, the music festival, is one I've not come across in any other westerns and it's this element that helps make this book so unique. George G. Gilman (author Terry Harknett) must have had fun coming up with the singers and band names that are to play at the High Mountain festival, people and groups such as Rollo Stone, The Alice Cooper Choir and Robert Dillon. It's not only these names that made me smile, but so too did the sheriff's nickname, High-Fy, and the many other mentions of records and stereos. And then there's the Devil's Disciples who are obviously modelled on the Hell's Angels, and of course it's these that get on Edge's wrong side. Edge's run in with two of them, whilst attempting to take his horse across the street, provides one of the most memorable scenes of the book. Another unforgettable

character is that of Hiram Rydell, an Easterner who talks like he's stepped out of a dime novel, who is soon acting, speaking and killing much like Edge, which greatly disturbs the half-breed.

As is to be expected from a George G. Gilman book the story is written in a hard-boiled style, filled with savage and brutally descriptive violence, and includes many groan-worthy one-liners from Edge.

Rhapsody in Red is one of my favourite entries in the Edge series.

GRINGOS #5: EASY MONEY
By J.D. Sandon
Mayflower, 1979

In this case the pseudonym of J.D. Sandon being shared by Angus Wells and John Harvey, the former being the author behind this book. The series ran for ten books.

So just who are the Gringos?
Cade Onslow: US Army Major. Deserter, with nothing to gain but vengeance.
Jonas Strong: Top Sergeant, damned by his colour.
Yates McCloud: Rapist. Nowhere to go but hell.
Jamie Durham: The needle of morphine was the only answer to his ruined face.
Four men with nothing left to lose but their lives. And they didn't count for much in the bloody fury of rebellion.

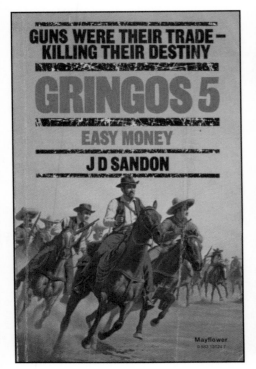

This entry into the series finally reveals the identity of the man who has been pursuing the Gringos throughout the series, making this a not to be missed book for followers of series.

Even though the Gringos begin to suspect all is not as it seems they still ride into the trap set for them. On their journey they gather a group of bandits together to help with their task of stealing the howitzers. Their trail to Tampico proves to be a dangerous and very bloody path. In fact almost from the word go this book seems to be one very violent struggle until its end.

Angus Wells includes a superbly written, and very visual, escape

from Tampico aboard a train which doesn't go quite according to plan and sees one of them fall into the hands of enemy. This allows Wells to add some brutal torture scenes to the story before the other Gringos fight their way in to free the captive, and then blast their way out again.

Wells also manages to further develop the relationship between the four men, especially that of Strong and McCloud, the latter being a Southerner who doesn't particularly like riding alongside a man of colour.

Wells adds a neat twist to the end of the story that leaves a question mark over the worth of the mission and the cost in human life.

If you've enjoyed other series written by the Piccadilly Cowboys then I'd think you should enjoy this series too, even though it is set in a time period a little later than many might consider a true western.

GUNSLINGER #2: THE GOLDEN GUN
as by Charles C. Garrett
Sphere, 1978

After his father's death in the first book of the series, Ryker is at a loss as what to do with himself, and this is when he finds himself tricked by the fat lawman, Nolan, to head out on the bounty trail. This provides some great reading about Ryker's self-doubts about his abilities to be a bounty hunter due to his lack of experience in hunting outlaws, and of using guns in anger.

Each of the Gunslinger books features a different gun, and all the books contain loads of information about guns; in this case it's a standard Dragoon that Ryker will work on to turn into a work of art. How he does this is all explained in fascinating detail.

Once Muerta double-crosses Ryker you know you're in for a bloodbath as Ryker takes on the whole gang single-handedly. All the killing described in gory detail as only Angus Wells can. (Charles C. Garrett is a pseudonym shared by Wells and Laurence James)

Like most of the books to come from the group of writers known as the Piccadilly Cowboys, there are plenty of references to their other series heroes. In this case in the form of memories of them calling into Ryker's gunsmith store.

For me, this was always one of the best in the series, and I'd recommend it to anyone who has an interest in guns of the west and likes their westerns filled with savage, bloody action.

HART THE REGULATOR #4: THE SILVER LIE
by John B. Harvey
Pan, 1980

The first part of this book sees Hart trying to find a friend who appeared in the previous book and also mentions quite a few events that happened in that book and those before. Because of this I'll suggest new readers to the series may find it worthwhile reading the first three books before reading this one.

Once Hart is persuaded to escort Alice to Denver the story really picks up in pace. John Harvey also spends a lot of time fleshing out the Sternberg gang; telling us their backgrounds and reasons for riding the outlaw trail. In fact Hart isn't in this part of the book much. When he is it is usually showing him at odds with Alice, which leads to some humorous dialogue.

Although the violence isn't described in as much gory detail as the other writers might have done, who shared the name of the Piccadilly Cowboys, it nevertheless is as brutal at times.

This book also introduces the reader to a character who will play an important part in Hart's life in a later book.

As I've said this book is perhaps not as savage as other work from the Piccadilly Cowboys, so as well as being essential reading for their fans, this should appeal to all who enjoy a fast-moving action-packed tale.

HAWK #9:
THE WIDOWMAKER
By William S. Brady
Fontana, 1981

The Hawk series first appeared in 1979 and ran for fifteen books, the last one coming out in 1983. William S. Brady being a pseudonym shared by Angus Wells and John Harvey, this entry being written by Wells.

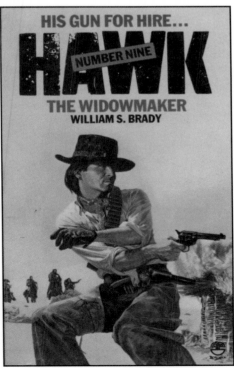

Like most anti-heroes created by the group of authors known as The Piccadilly Cowboys, Jared Hawk is a cold, heartless, character who can be every bit as cruel as those he is hunting, and the book has its fair share of savage violence told in all its gory detail.

Wells includes a number of short

flashback sequences to explain some of Hawk's past, in particular why he wears a black glove on his left hand and of his time working with John T. McLain (the lead character from another William S. Brady series; Peacemaker).

Like many PC heroes Hawk carries an unusual weapon, a cut-down Meteor single barrel shotgun, carried in a specially designed belt holster, and this gun is used to devastating effect.

The story itself gets off to a good start but then seems to plod on as much of the rest of the book is taken up with Hawk tracking the kidnappers, with nothing much happening, although Wells' descriptions of landscapes and conditions are very well told.

> HAWK IS A COLD, HEARTLESS, CHARACTER WHO CAN BE EVERY BIT AS CRUEL AS THOSE HE IS HUNTING, AND THE BOOK HAS ITS FAIR SHARE OF SAVAGE VIOLENCE TOLD IN ALL ITS GORY DETAIL

Once Hawk finds the truth behind the kidnapping he decides to take matters into his own hands and the book comes to a blood drenched conclusion.

Perhaps not the best work to come from Angus Wells but still worth a look if your preferred choice in western reading is for the more brutal books.

HERNE THE HUNTER #11: SILVER THREADS
as by John J. McLaglen
Corgi, 1979

John J. McLaglen is a pseudonym shared by Laurence James and John Harvey. This book was written by Laurence James.

The Sowren sisters make for two very memorable characters, James paints a gentle image of them, then through hints and finally actions brings out their real personalities in a series of shocking revelations, including sadistic torture and other perversions. These two elements often turn up in books written by James, but by having them as the darker side of two sweet old ladies, helps make them two of the most memorable characters James created.

Silver Threads also contains an equally memorable challenge to Herne's reputation as a fast gun. The shootist trying to avoid the confrontation, even though he knows what the inevitable outcome will be. This scene is beautifully captured by the cover artist right down to the correct colour clothing.

For me, Silver Threads has always been one of the strongest entries in the Herne the Hunter series, and re-reading it now, confirms this is still so.

If you like tough, brutal, westerns then this book is well worth checking out – as is the whole series in my opinion. After Edge, Herne the Hunter is my favourite series to come from the group of authors known as the Piccadilly Cowboys.

IF YOU LIKE TOUGH, BRUTAL, WESTERNS THEN THIS BOOK IS WELL WORTH CHECKING OUT – AS IS THE WHOLE SERIES IN MY OPINION

THE LAWMEN #2:
KANSAS BLOODY KANSAS
as by J.B. Dancer
Coronet 1977

Lee Fisher, Emma Wright and Brad McGarry make up the team of Lawmen featured in this series.

The Lawmen are hired to tackle Missouri Raiders. As America rushes into Civil War other people see the coming war as a way to riches. Lee Fisher and Emma infiltrate the whilst McGarry heads for Northville.

Fisher has to be tested to be accepted into the gang and this involves killing people he's here to protect. This only succeeds in fuelling the bitter hatred he has for the Raiders.

Emma struggles with her emotions too, fighting her attraction to Fisher who's made it very plain he likes her. McGarry plays a waiting

game, waiting to spring a trap in Northville.

But nothing is straightforward. Fisher is exposed as a spy. McGarry finds no one willing or able to stand with him in Northville. The Raiders ride for the town to destroy it completely.

This book builds in increasing pace to the final showdown in the town of Northville. The writing is confident and gripping but for those who've read many westerns the story doesn't really offer anything new. Having said that Kansas, Bloody Kansas is an entertaining read. As is expected from a book written by a member of the Piccadilly Cowboys (this time Angus Wells) there is plenty of brutal, graphic violence.

PEACEMAKER #5:
BLOOD RUN
as by William S. Brady
Fontana, 1982

The Peacemaker series lasted for nine books with six of them being written by Angus Wells and the other three by John Harvey. These two authors also wrote another series together as by William S. Brady: Hawk.

The two series are linked more than just by the author pseudonym. The Hawk series came first and

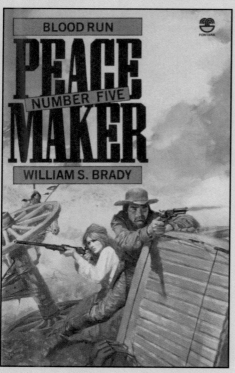

there's often mention of John T. McLain as being the man who helped Jared Hawk learn to handle weapons, in fact he gave Hawk the swan-down Meteor shotgun he wears in a special belt holster. There were always rumours of the two starring in a book together, sadly this never happened as the English publishers ceased publishing westerns before it could happen.

The Peacemaker series differed from the majority of the Piccadilly Cowboy's western series in that it didn't feature a drifting hero. After the end of the Civil War, McLain rides into the small town of Garrison and stays. The books follow the growth of this town and also feature a cast of regular characters. This allowed the authors to spend time developing these people as well as the town. Each book begins with prologue filling new readers in on the main details of what had happened in the previous books.

As the blurb indicates this story revolves around attempts to link Garrison with other towns by stage. It's not just Comanche that cause problems, there's bandits too, being helped by a greedy solider who sees the payroll the stage is carrying as an easy way to riches.

This entry in the series comes from Angus Wells so the violence is extremely detailed and gory. Having said that there is not as much as in some of Wells' books. Much of this story tells what the various characters are doing, how they are planning to steal the payroll and double-cross each other. All this leads to an exciting final bloody confrontation between all sides.

One thing that always made me smile about this series is that McLain rode with Bloody Bill Anderson, Butcher Harvey and Josey Wales throughout much of the Civil War, and that it was Wales that suggests McLain heads for Texas at the end of the war.

Blood Run reads like a fast moving traditional western except it contains a bit more blood and guts than those who've never read a western from this group of writers might expect. In my mind the Peacemaker series is definitely worth exploring…if you can find them.

ADAM STEELE #20: WANTED FOR MURDER

as by George G. Gilman
NEL, April 1979

George G. Gilman (Terry Harknett) has written a terrific story in *Wanted for Murder*. His two plotlines twist together in what seems to be an impossible situation for Adam Steele to escape from a free man – or even with his life.

There is plenty of time for Steele to reflect upon his reasons for taking

another's life, as he can relate to the need for vengeance, even though he remains coldly indifferent to the agonizing story behind the assassination attempt. And it's the fact he only kills to satisfy his own need for revenge, or if he's in a life or death confrontation, that provides the fascination of this story, that keeps the reader turning the pages to see if Adam Steele can talk, or fight, his way out of having to pull the trigger.

> IT CONTAINS A BIT MORE BLOOD AND GUTS THAN THOSE WHO'VE NEVER READ A WESTERN FROM THIS GROUP OF WRITERS MIGHT EXPECT

George G. Gilman has a reputation for writing books filled with death and gruesome scenes of descriptive killing, and rightly so in many cases – particularly in his earlier work. The death toll isn't high in this book, Steele only killing one person - although that's not the only death within the story. The book is filled with a number of brutal scenes as the tough characters, of both sexes, engage in a gripping battle of wits and nerve. There are a couple of superbly written, tension filled, chase sequences, that'll keep the reader turning the pages.

If you're a fan of tough, gritty westerns then this is a book not to be missed.

I must also give credit to Tony Masero, for painting such a superb cover for this book, probably my favourite of the entire Adam Steele series.

CALEB THORN #4: BLOODY SHILOH
By L.J. Coburn
Sphere, 1978

L.J. Coburn is a pseudonym used by two authors, Laurence James and John Harvey, and the latter wrote this book. Caleb Thorn is the shortest series written by the The Piccadilly Cowboys.

I always thought it was a shame there weren't more of them, but at the time I read a quote from an author (possibly from Terry Harknett) who said writing a western series set in the America Civil War would be a financial disaster. Strange when you consider that the Caleb Thorn series must have been born from the fan praise for Harknett's own Civil War flashback sequences in his highly successful Edge series written as George G. Gilman. But then again as Caleb Thorn only made it to five books then perhaps he was right?

As well as having its origins in those Edge Civil War books, this series also seems to borrow from the film *The Dirty Dozen*, in as much as the small group of soldiers that Caleb rides with are all vicious criminals saved from an immediate death sentence to fight for the Union.

The books are extremely violent, and all of Thorn's Raid-

read for followers of the series.

The rest of this story is fairly routine, and other than the Caroline Jansen storyline, doesn't offer any surprises, even the identity of the traitor is easy to work out. Having said that the book is an entertaining read with extremely well written battle sequences.

Fans of the Piccadilly Cowboy's work should not miss this book, indeed this series, if you can find them today as they are some of the harder PC books to find. Anyone else who enjoys books set in the American Civil War and/or westerns of the more brutal kind should consider picking this one up if you're lucky enough to find a copy.

ers, including Caleb, take pleasure from killing Rebels – or anyone else who gets in their way. Throughout the series a number of story threads continue from book to book, and *Bloody Shiloh* sees a grudging respect form between Thorn and his commanding officer, Lieutenant-Colonel Jansen - Thorn killed Jansen's son in a duel and is thus hated by both Jansen and his wife. This story also develops Thorn's relationship with Caroline Jansen, one that will lead to a bloody moment of madness that will have dire consequences for all involved, making this book a must

THE UNDERTAKER #4: THREE GRAVES TO A SHOWDOWN
By George G. Gilman
NEL, January 1982

Barnaby Gold, The Undertaker, is perhaps George G. Gilman's coldest character, a man who will stop at nothing to achieve his aims, as he points out during this story, there are 'just two kinds of men I kill. Those that are trying to kill me. And those that get in the way of me doing what I want to do.'

Gilman includes enough back-story to fill in those who haven't read the previous books to explain why Gold has a ten-thousand-dollar bounty on his head, which in turn enlightens new readers as to what drives the man known as The Undertaker towards the final confrontation he engineers, and this is done in a macabre style that makes for a dramatic last showdown.

The Undertaker is, perhaps, Gilman's least known western series, coming some years after Edge and Adam Steele. This, the fourth book was meant to be the last and the ending certainly reads like it could have been, and for me would have made for an excellent conclusion to the series, but the publisher persuaded the author to write two more.

Like Edge with the razor he carries behind his neck and Steele with his stick-pin and thugee scarf, Barnaby Gold has an unusual weapon, a swivel Peacemaker, and he also has another gimmick; his screw together shovel that he uses to bury all those he kills, in fact insists on doing so.

FILLED WITH TOUGH-TALKING AND ACTING CHARACTERS THIS STORY RACES ALONG AT GREAT PACE.

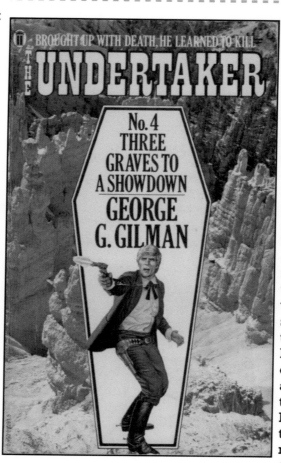

BROUGHT UP WITH DEATH, HE LEARNED TO KILL

THE UNDERTAKER

No. 4
THREE GRAVES TO A SHOWDOWN
GEORGE G. GILMAN

Filled with tough-talking and acting characters this story races along at great pace, offering a couple of surprising revelations along the way. For those who have read the other Gilman series', you'll find less of the groan inducing puns, and the graphic violence somewhat toned down, but that is not a criticism in any way for this book is highly entertaining and a must read for all Gilman fans.

OUT OF THE BLACK SHADOWS OF HELL

CROW
BY JUSTIN MARRIOTT

Crow lasted only eight episodes at Corgi from 1979 to 1982, but in that short time he more than lived up to his back cover billing of being the "meanest son of a bitch ever".

Devoid of restraint and surface-level irony, Crow could well be either the most or least humorous western series of all time. In the opening chapter of debut *The Red Hills (1979)*, Crow's trademark yellow bandana (he's otherwise dressed head to toe in black) is stolen by a loveable mongrel dog owned by a little girl- cue lisp, freckles and blonde curls. When the girl's increasingly frantic calls to her pet fail to secure the return of his bandana, Crow promptly uses his sawn-off double-barrelled Meteor shot-gun to blast the dog into tatters of flesh. To a nation of animal lovers, I can't imagine a more effective way of announcing that your character isn't going to play by the rules!

It is noteworthy that another James-authored cowboy series featured the anti-hero finishing off a character's pet-dog. I wonder if this was James' blackly comic response to George Gilman, his great friend, revealing the complaints he received for killing a dog in the Edge series?

Laurence James, that most mischievous of the Piccadilly Cowboys, was the capable pen behind the James Marvin pseudonym credited on the Crow books; a pop culture Magpie James loved to lace his western anti-heroes with industrial strength doses of masochism and brutality, and to shock his reader's with kinky excess.

He certainly doesn't let the fur settle in *The Red Hills*,

with Crow soon knee-deep in conflict with an alcoholic cavalry officer who has sent his unfaithful wife to her certain doom at the hands of a tribe of scalp-happy natives. From his own carnal encounter with the lady Crow is aware of her very luxuriant pubic hair, which he later spies in the scalp collec-

CORGI

Out of the black shadows of Hell comes

CROW 5

JAMES W. MARVIN

BODY GUARD

tion of a sadistic Indian! That old joke springs to mind – "What is that in white chalk behind me?" "That is THE line…"

In the second book, *Worse than Death* (1979), a titular reference to the fate of anyone taken prisoner by the Apache, a cavalry battalion make the mistake of kidnapping the young son of a local chief and soon find themselves behind a stockade of wagons, besieged by angry braves. Crow is part of this band which becomes so depleted only he and the wives of the soldiers and the chief's son are left. Weak and starving after days without supplies (although with enough energy to engage in a bout of group sex), Crow is forced to venture beyond their stockade to scout for food and provisions. Returning empty-handed, Crow discover that in his absence the women had given into their hunger….

"Very tender, it was," interrupted Martha Hetherington. "We've stripped most of the meat off to dry. We flayed the head."

They showed him what remained of the young Shoshone boy. A scattering of bloody bones and a raw skull, the eyes milky and staring in their sockets. The ribs had been hacked away with a heavy cleaver and all the soft flesh from the inside

of the arms and legs cut neatly off with a sharp knife."

Crow's sole mission is self-preservation, a credo that is constantly tested by his habit of finding himself trapped between bloodthirsty Indian warriors, devious cavalry officers and their half-witted conscripts. When not shacking up with cannibalistic sex-fiends, his adventures are played out in a bitter landscape of torrential rain or bitter cold that makes spit crackle and freeze be-fore it hits the ground. Crow's origin is shrouded in mystery, hinting that as well as serving in the cavalry, he has spent time with the Native Americans.

CROW'S ORIGIN IS SHROUDED IN MYSTERY HINTING HE HAS SPENT TIME WITH THE NATIVE AMERICANS

The normal in-jokes abound, with the pseudonyms used by fellow Piccadilly Cowboys turning up in characters such as Frank Chandler (Terry Harknett) John McLaglen (James himself) and James Muir (Angus Wells). Bob Tanner, who was head honcho at New English Library who

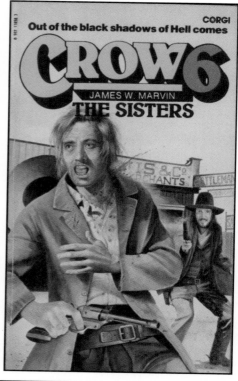

was oil to James's water when working as an editor at the publisher, gets a real lambasting as a particularly shoddy cavalry man- "No great loss at the best of times but in a situation like this even Tanner would have been better than nobody"!

There are also guest appearances from Herne, with Crow making several references to his oft-stated catch-phrase of "Have you ever been stung by a dead bee?". There are also veiled references to Crow knowing Edge, although he is never named due to copyright reasons.

With the cannibalism, torture and kinky sex, this is as O.T.T. as any western series gets (certainly for the UK, although I have yet to read the Kilburn series written by Morris Hershman as Sam Victor for Manor Books in the US) and I can't imagine how James could have made it any more extreme. Knowing there was a sly grin and a dark sense of humour behind the excess does grant the series a certain sleazy charm.

However, much like the Herne series covered elsewhere in this issue, this is more of a western series for those that don't like westerns.

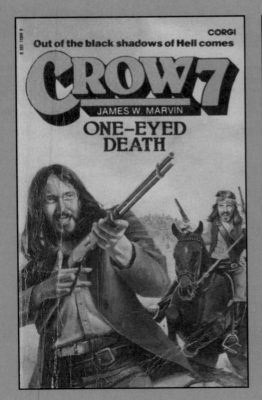

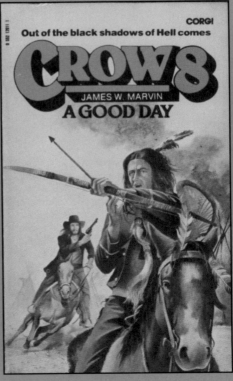

A GOLD STRIKE OF WESTERN LORE

WESTERN MAGAZINE
BY PAUL BISHOP

In October 1980, the slick size *Western Magazine* debut in the British newsagents and the first Western genre information magazine was born. Western Magazine's godhead of consultants Mike Stotter and David Whitehead, and editor Dennis Winston were determine to produce the kind of genre magazine they themselves would want to read.

Today, longtime school friends Whitehead (aka: Ben Bridges) and Stotter are best-selling Western writers themselves. They are also the dynamic duo behind Piccadilly Publishing, which has given new life in ebook form some of the most popular and best-loved Western and action-adventure series fiction of the last forty years. But in 1980, as struggling writers, they idolized the group of British writers known as The Piccadilly Cowboys. These hard living word-slingers had introduced new life into the staid Western genre with ultra-violent stories of six-gun justice and unrepentant anti-heroes. **Western Magazine** was a vehicle to unite the vast audience of Western fans

by providing a monthly wealth of related Western articles and reviews—and exclusive stories from the most popular Western series of the day.

Prior to **Western Magazine** there had been a number of Western fiction digests such as **Luke Short Westerns, Zane Gray's Western Magazine**, and **Louis L'Amour Western Magazine**. These were strictly Western fiction only vehicles trading on the best-selling Western Writ-

----

WHAT ISSUES THEY WERE,
FILLED TO THE BRIM WITH
EVERYTHING FOR WHICH A
FAN OF WESTERNS COULD
ASK

ers' names on their masthead. *Western Magazine* was refreshingly different.

Each issue of *Western Magazine* included stories from the mega-popular Western writers Whitehead and Stotter revered. New stories featuring Edge, Herne the Hunter, Morgan Kane, Breed, Bodie the Stalker, Steele, Hart the Regulator, and Sudden gave **Western Magazine** something very special.

There were many other non-fiction articles featuring the guns that tamed the West, bloodthirsty Indian Tribes, real-life desperados, and overviews of other popular characters in Western fiction. There was even a beautiful pull-out poster of Annie Oakley for those who found **Playboy** centre-folds too tame.

Starting a new magazine of any kind is an exercise in tilting at windmills and, unfortunately, **Western Magazine** bit the dust at High Noon on Main Street after only four issue. But what issues they were, filled to the brim with everything for which a fan of Westerns could ask. Copies of the original four issues occasionally show up on e-Bay (where I found mine), but prices can range from reasonable to ridiculous. But **Western Magazine** is the holy grail for many collectors, with good reason. My own fan boy *what if* fantasy is having ten, twenty, or a hundred issues of **Western Magazine** to find and collect—a gold strike of Western lore like no other.

FLYING LEAD

I hope you've enjoyed this premier issue of **Hot Lead**, which could well be the first fanzine dedicated to vintage western paperbacks. I'm sure some purists will tell me that vintage means pre-60s, but in this case, I would apply the label vintage to pretty much any western published before 1985.

Although I don't necessarily consider myself a dyed-in-the-wool fan of the western paperback – I just enjoy any quality pulp fiction irrespective of genre- I have long admired its longevity. Fads and fashions come and go in popular fiction, but the western keeps on riding. And that is what I find so fascinating and beguiling about the genre, and plan to celebrate in these pages.

As I am not an expert in the field, I've tried to fill the pages of this zine with people who are. Paul Bishop, who recently co-edited the excellent book *52 Weeks • 52 Western Novels*, is on board as Ghost Editor and contributor. Paul's enthusiasm was key in moving **Hot Lead** from a whimsy into a living breathing publication with a vision and a plan. I am delighted that his series of articles on the development of the modern western in paperback will typically open each issue.

Another expert is Steve Myall whose long-running Western Fiction Reviews blog is a must-read. Remember the catch-phrase from the classic pulp radio show – "The Shadow Knows"? Well I lost count of the number of times a question regarding an obscure western series or title posed on various FB groups would be answered by someone volunteering, "Steve Myall knows." So pleased to have Steve on board with his Cowpoke Critic column.

In the second issue – which is damned near complete and with a theme of "The Art of the Western" – will add Andreas Decker and Jim O'Brien to the mix of contributors. I look forward to welcoming them on board. And hopefully others.

My normal sounding boards told me it was a folly to launch a fanzine dedicated to westerns, and they could be right. I hope we can prove them wrong (in the nicest way, of course) and that **Hot Lead** can become a regular fixture.

Please spread the word through Facebook and by leaving reviews at Amazon – which don't need to be 5 Star (although of course that would be cool), just honest.

Justin

Printed in Great Britain
by Amazon